Unvoiced Love Seeks Affection

A Silent Heart's Journey Through Longing and Hope

Bharat Jangid

BLUEROSE PUBLISHERS
India | U.K.

For permissions requests or inquiries regarding this publication, please contact:

BLUEROSE PUBLISHERS
www.BlueRoseONE.com
info@bluerosepublishers.com
+91 8882 898 898
+4407342408967

ISBN: 978-93-7310-874-2

Cover Design: Shubham Verma
Typesetting: Sagar

First Edition: September 2025

Dedication

"To whom I love, and waiting
For acceptance,
Of my love by 'Him-Her '"

Bharat jangid

Acknowledgement

This book is a piece of my soul, and I would like to express my deepest gratitude to all those who supported me throughout the journey of writing this book. To my readers, your hearts were always in my thoughts as I wrote every word.

I owe my deepest gratitude to my parents Mr.Brijesh Kumar Sharma and Mrs.Suman Sharma for their endless support, patience and midnight pep talks.

I appreciate the guidance of my Professors Azhar Uddin Sahaji, Akansha goswami and Saumya shah. At Delhi University. Their lectures on poetry, history of literature and ways of using different vocabulary. Which provided me a lot of support and knowledge.

My heartfelt thanks to my Prof. Azhar Uddin Sahaji, who helped me a lot and no one knows and he also doesn't know that. Only because of him I was able to complete my book. With all my emotions, love and feelings.

Special thanks to my friends Chahat malhotra and Ankita for their support and encouragement in completing my book. And for different ideas and discussion with them.

Most importantly I thank the divine muse who helped me a lot after being disappeared from every eye and special thanks to Ratikanta who blessed me with love and emotions for "ONE" person that love and emotions I expressed in the book.

Preface

" Love's gift cannot be given, it waits to be accepted.":- Robindranath Tagore.

This quote from Tagore is all that can be said about the one-sided bond of love. Poetry, as the essence of an expression of art and literature, aesthetics and realism, belongs to the purest domain of creation. It has always been communication but more about those impressions which cannot be communicated. This ' non-communicable process contains the most intense of meanings, those experiences that are most elusive in words and real in living.

My tryst with poetry had been an ordinary one in the beginning. My poems are simple and elegant with use of different vocabulary.

These poems are about one-sided love and lop-sided bond. The poems are expressing

Condition of lover who is waiting for the love of his or her beloved.

These poems are expressing the sacred wall and eyes of society for the love of same gender and in different gender. The poems in this book completely relate with every one life and every one struggles with their hunger of love for their beloved.

To conclude, these poems are straight from my experiences and sensations that follow them. I convince my readers to create meanings and absurdities.Where I stop short. I wish my readers a great read.

Contents

One-Sided life without Love

When day transits into night__,
Thoughts of you always in my mind.
Coz have to face life without you__,
That gives me fear of losing sidedness of you.

Know very well that's not with me.
Coz can't able to express you.
Thoughts of you stucked in me.
Which always lives in sight of you.

Satan loves me more than you.
Coz he always gazes to kill at once,
But you kill me ten times in every hour.
Thoughts of you give blindness to my life.

People and Religion says,
That I am not perfect for your life,
In hopes loveless, I own you,
And you my one-sided life,
But this one-sidedness of love kills my love.

I live in you no one knows

From the morning till night,
I live in you my beloved light;
Like air which no one saw.
I merge into you whom no one knows;
I live among everyone's eyes.
But eyes always lives in your smile's;
I always live in you beyond everyone's eyes.

Society thinks I live alone,
My love knows we live as one;
"WE" is not you, but your memories,
With whom I live alone, beyond all boundaries;
Religion makes it tougher for me to live with you.
"It pleases religion, but not the soul",
They don't know I always live in and with you.

I die, But my love will not

O my dear,
You there, I here and I hear.
Your eyes rain like clouds,
And water touches my shroud.

I leave you thus alone-
The home where I lived, for all.
When you come, you will not be alone,
My presence will be there for you all.

In form of things-
Or in things like diamond rings,
Which I used to wear,
When it glints, I am always there.

If you miss me there,
Then see the verandah which is near-
Where I saw you growing every year.
Meanwhile for going when it late I always hear,
I will die, but not my love for you dear.

Fear to "Express" love

You and me live always near,
Then also I have fear;
After expressing love for you,
Fear of losing you.

Infront of you I live in yearning-
-for expressing my love meaning.
For me your presence,
Always acts like absence.

I know you do this deliberately,
For tormenting me purposely;
Then also I love you "With Fear",
Due to this freaking society seer;

You know how much I pray for you,
"Pray" of not losing you-
This "Losing" for me is fear-
"Fear" in expressing my love for you " DEAR ".

To whom should I say I love you

When I decided to tell you,
" FEAR " enters at the thought of losing you.
My love always lives in your sight,
And my " SIGHT " seeks your love's side.

When I spoke to God.
About my love for you.
He replied to see the limits of religion,
Before making any decision.

I told my dear ones about you,
But they criticise my love for you;
This society is SATAN,
Always devouring me like " SEITAN ".

I confess to myself about you,
That **I LOVE YOU.**
Beyond all boundaries,
Ignoring everyone around me.

I love you through all,
Your phases of life,
But to whom should,
I say " **I LOVE YOU**".

My tears ask me why they are

Everyone sees me smiling,
But no one knows I'm crying;
Two eyes, in which tears arise.
Both ask each other,
For whom and why they are.

One said I'm crying because of love,
Other said I'm crying because of your absence.
But both don't know,
That they are because of you.
You know everything yet,
You ignore me;

Two eyes two different tears arise,
One shows religion and the other shows society;
Both question each other why they are.
Society says it's because of fear of expressing love;
Religion says it's because of boundaries I made.
Both don't know that they are related to you,
For your love,
And;
My tears, ask me why they are.

Rain depicts my Emotions

Rain always falls outside but,
It shows my heaviness from inside.
Rainwater falls from clouds,
And merges into rivers.

My dignity falls for your love,
And merges into my loneliness.
Cloud knows water will leave,
But then that is called Rainfall.

I know that you aren't with me,
But still waterfalls from my eyes.
This rain of eyes,
Depicts my emotions.

The cloud has a reason to cry,
I don't have that.
The cloud has a bond of water before it falls.
While we are always in front of each other.
But we do not have a bond of love.
And my emotions falls in form of,
Tears for that bond of our love–.

Love has no Gender, Religion, Future or Society

Loving the same gender is not a,
transgression.
Loving the same gender is the purest,
form of affection.
Because loving the same gender has,
No foresight except adoration.
I am loving someone knowing I have,
No future with him.
But still, I will love him.

I love him, but he is stuck within the,
Boundaries of religion.
Society labels me as QUEER, yet I still,
Love him.
I know loving the same gender has an,
Unwanted end, yet I love him.
I love him by dismissing gender, society,
And religion.

I know I have no future with, but,
Loving you is not my sin.
My love for you is not confined to,
Any gender, religion, society or future.
My love is pure feeling for you.
The only insecurity I have is the-
-fear of losing you.

Even after my death, I will love you.
My love is not simply affection for you,
I will dedicate myself to you.
I know loving the same gender is,
Not a transgression but a pure,
Form of love towards one's beloved.

Rising sun rises a hope

Rising sun rises a hope.
In my heart to express you,
My love for you my Beloved.

Rising sun rises a hope.
In my heart that,
The wait is near end.
In living lopsided bond,
With silent affection.

Rising sun rises a hope.
In my heart that,
The day arrived,
When I will be your's,
My heart's desire.

Rising sun rises a hope.
In my heart that,
My thirst for closeness,
Is over; My love and me,
Is in your perception.

Rising sun rises a hope.
In my heart that,
The crimson guilt of being,
Silent in front of you.
It will be over today.

By saying you something,
My dearest cherished soul,
That I LOVE YOU my precious.

Rising sun rises a hope.
In my heart—-.

My emotions are trapped in my heart

My emotions are trapped in my heart.
My crimson core stucked in those.
They are in my soul chamber.
I can't let them out,
Coz I am afraid of losing you.

My emotions are trapped in my heart.
Those are of my moonlight soul.
Searching for an echo of silent comfort.
Those are mine better half to ——----
——------ whom I CAN TALK.

My emotions are TRAPPED in my heart.
Those are the rain behind my eyes.
Inner tide of silent ocean.
Which always reminds me.
My love yearning for you.

My emotions are TRAPPED in my heart.
Those are WINGLESS flights.
Wants their expression of admiration.
But have great fear——----------
——-------- of LOSING YOU. Dear.

Until how Long

Until how long—-
My heart questions me.
I will live with,
A silent commitment.

Until how long—-
You will ignore me.
Due to sacred divides and,
Faith-bound limits.

Until how long—-
I will ignore the naked reality,
Of living in lopsided passion.
Because of your spiritual gulf.

Until how long—-
I have to face,
The eyes of the world.
Who always says me that,
I did wrong after being in,
Eternal flame.

Until how long—-
My love hungover faces stillness in motion.
My inner blaze is praying for,
Our closeness.

Until how long—
I have to put my affection,
Under emotional weight with,
Crushing silence,
Of unspoken devotion and,
Moral scaffolding.

Until how long—
I myself don't know.

Why can't we live together

I always ask you–
Why can't we live together?
You says that this inseparability,
Would be judged by,
The eyes of the world.

I always ask you–
Why can't we live together?
You say that the,
Generation gap is the,
Main cause.

I always ask you–
Why can't we live together?
You say that you are,
Tied to ancestral roots,
And dogmatic chains with doctrinal walls.

I always ask you–
Why can't we live together?
You say that serenity would wounded,
By hollow silence of,
Half-built bond.

I always ask you–
Why can't we live together?
You say that our unspoken yearning,
Will burn in bitter fire of,
Traditional norms and public judgement.

I always ask you–
Why can't we live together?

In seeking you, I lost myself

I lost myself.
In search of you and your love.
In nameless ocean of souls you are–
The light in the void,for me.
In seas of faces I misplaced myself.

I search you in social circles.
Of unfamiliar multitude in,
In mass of wandering spirits.
In search of you and your love.
I lost myself in the cold fury of culture.

I search you in monasteries.
I believe god, he will help me in-
Searching of you my love a infinite,
Yearning of my life.
I lost myself in monasteries,
Of spiritual gulf.

I search you in cage of norms,
In the eyes of the world but from them,
I received shadows of bitterness.
I lost myself.
In search of you and your love.

What is my Fault

One day I asked myself.
What is my fault?
Did I do anything wrong,
By loving you my heart's desire.

One day I asked my-
Sheltering arms and trust bearers.
Having emotional intimacy,
With my beloved why does it,
Always gives me wounds.
What is my fault in that ?

Desiring someone and,
Loving someone is a feeling.
That takes birth in me and others,
Charaiveti-Charaiveti, till we live.
What is my fault in that ?

The burning resentment of,
Judgemental eyes,
And sacred doctrines kills me,
Shanai-Shanai everyday.
I love you; what is my fault in that ?

This burden of blame with cultural cage,
And divine belief questions me,
Why do I love someone of the same gender,
And from another religion.
But I love you.
What is my fault in that ?

One day I asked myself:
What is my fault,
In loving you ?

The other side of One-Sided Love

Love has two sides,
One-sided love and,
Love from both sides.
People who are in,
One-sided love always have,
Silence in their love life.
About which no one knows.

That side of silence in,
One sided love.
Is a promise of tomorrow,
And shows an unfulfilled,
Dream of a lover

That side of silence in,
One-sided love.
Reflects the silent prayer,
For the union of souls,
And the delicate wish,
Of lovers' confessions.

That side of silence in,
One-sided love.
Gives wounds without,
Scars everyday to the,
Lover who is in hope of,
Acceptance in the arms of his lover,
Till he is dying everyday.

That side of silence in,
One-sided love.
Reflects limitless devotion,
Beyond every "NO" and the spiritual,
Divide with a cultural cage,
And the hope of being chosen.

That side of silence in,
One-sided love.
Reflects the soul's smile and,
Inner sunshine that one day,
He will be accepted by,
His lover.

Unilateral bond of Love

Love is a pure feeling,
Of our hearts.
That gives glory and glow,
To the face.
Love can also be disastrous,
If a person is in,
A unilateral bond of love.

A unilateral bond of love,
In anyone's life.
Is like a boundless void,
Without hope,
Of expressing love.

A unilateral bond of love,
In anyone's life.
Is like a seasonless tree,
And life without joyless festivity,
With unending openness.

A unilateral bond of love,
In anyone's life.
Is like wisdom without echo,
And art without soul,
Life is like lifeless soil.

Not everyone gets the same,
Glory and glow to their faces.
Sometimes love gives paleness,
To the face and makes,
Life a womb of dust.

But this unilateral,
Bond of love is,
The only hope of unity,
Amidst every hope—--.

Tale of Rain and Eyes

Eyes questions to rain,
WHY are you falling down?
Rain replies,
WHY are you falling down?

Eyes replied,
Because of unspoken love and,
Unexpressed love,
For my Beloved.
And because,
Suppressed by the eyes of the world

Rain replies,
Me too, this is not,
Simple rainwater, but-
My tears.
Because of losing the bond with the cloud.

Intimacy of Unshared Emotions

One who is hope-rooted soul,
Is like a blooming flower.
Before it grows completely,
Everyone plucks it.
Same is like with feather-souled,
Everyone kills him.

Unshared emotions have a,
Kind of unexpressed intimacy.
In which person becomes,
Yearning soul and kind to the core.

Kind soul always lives in,
Unending wait.
Of getting love of their beloved,
But they get quietless world.

One who is living with,
Unshared emotions.
They live without desire,
They don't want sacred touch,
Lustful lullaby or sexual intercourse,
They just need the love of their beloved.

Fire and Water or An Unexpressed Love

Fire is you,
And water is me.
Everyone knows that,
Both can't be one for,
Forever.

When water tested by time to enter,
With bravery beneath fear,
Within the aura of flame.
Fire vanishes and give water,
A cloak of emptiness with,
Soundless scream.

I am,
Water.
Without pause I receive,
Shadows all around with realm of fears,
And quiet chaos from Beloved.

Four white walls surrounded me, the sky is my only Hope

Four white walls caged me.
Each wall is painted,
With different invisible colours.
Which I can only see,
Not anyone else can see those colours.

Wall of my frontside.
Painted with colour of religion,
Like Saffron, Green, Blue And Gold.
And questions me silently,
That how I will cross the,
Sacred barrier and divine boundary,
For you my love.

My rightside wall.
Painted with colour of Queer,
Black and White, Red, Brown and Beige.
Their unseen eyes without any pause,
Gazes me for questioning my gender,
Sex and character.

My leftside wall.
Painted with Pale Yellow, Faded Red and,
Black colour.
Which is the scent of your,
Memory.
And always gives me nostalgia,
Of past days with you.

The wall at my backside.
Painted with Bright Red, Lovely Pink and,
Fresh Natured Green colour.
The wall at my backside.
Always encourages me to tell you,
My love yearning for you,
And to express my love in front of you.

The roof wall.
Painted with Royal Blue and White colour.
This open sky is my only hope.
Which gives me breath of tomorrow,
That you will accept me and my love.

I confess my love for you, Dear

Yes, I pour my heart,
With you,
Into sacred bond.
You are my boundless yearning.
Above all worldly rules.
I confess my love for you, DEAR.

My sacred muse,
You are my whole universe,
And never imagine a moment,
Without you.
And my life halts,
Without your name.
I confess my love for you, DEAR.

All I know is you,
I can mute the world for you.
You are my silent prayer,
For whom I always pray,
And can be a prey.
I confess my love for you, DEAR.

Not even time can erase,
And sacred walls can stop.
My tender madness for you,
My heart's monarch.
Beyond breath-beyond reason,
And greater than time or fate,
I love you more than forever.
I confess my love for you, DEAR.

All I know is that,
You wrap me into your truth,
Fold me into your breath,
And melt me in your embrace.
You are my need not my want,
You are my whole universe,
You are my every dawn and dusk,
To whom I love above all holy lines,
And above worldly rules.
You are my heart's echo and,
My whole universe.
I confess my love for you, DEAR.
I LOVE YOU,
I LOVE YOU,
I LOVE YOU—.